I0136454

Anonymous

A Second Letter to the Common Council of the City of

London

Anonymous

A Second Letter to the Common Council of the City of London

ISBN/EAN: 9783337124731

Printed in Europe, USA, Canada, Australia, Japan

Cover: Foto ©Suzi / pixelio.de

More available books at **www.hansebooks.com**

A

SECOND LETTER

TO THE

COMMON COUNCIL

OF THE

CITY of LONDON,

WITH

Remarks on Lord Chief Juſtice PRATT's Anſwer to Sir THOMAS HARRISON the Chamberlain.

Litteras tuas legimus, ſimilimas edicti tui, contu-
meliofas, minaces, minimé dignas quæ a te mit-
terentur.   Cic. Epiſt. ad Anton.

LONDON:

Printed for W. NICOLL, at the Paper-mill,
in St. Paul's Church-yard.

MDCCLXIV.

A

SECOND LETTER

TO THE

COMMON COUNCIL

OF THE

CITY of LONDON.

GENTLEMEN,

THE proceedings of your vene-
rable body have, of late espe-
cially, been of so extraordinary
a nature, that you cannot, I am sure,
be surprized, at the notice and at-
tention with which even the minutest
circumstances relating to you are considered by the generality of your fellow
citizens :

B

citizens : what tho' the fubjects of your
important deliberations, are not fo much
as ventured to be gueffed at, yet even the
day and hour of your fittings, occafion
many nice fpeculations and fearful alarms ?
For my part, I own freely, though I
am not naturally more timid than any
other of his majefty's loving fubjects, yet
I could not help feeling the moft ferious
anxiety, upon reading in the news papers
(thofe impartial and unerring oracles, and
which in future times will be the faithful records of your fame to the lateft
pofterity) the following paragraph, *It is
expected that there will be a full court of
common council to-morrow at Guildhall,
and the lord mayor intends taking the chair
precifely at eleven o'clock, as it is faid feveral affairs of confequence will be taken
into confideration.* I began immediately
to reflect with myfelf what could pof-
fibly be the intention of fummoning this
court. I knew very well that all the ordinary

dinary bufinefs had been difpatched, the courts of confervacy, that is, as I have ever underftood them, the conferving or keeping up the laudable cuftom of good eating and drinking, had been already regularly held both at Stains and Barking; and it was too early in the year for fwan-hopping : there would have been no doubt, in that cafe, of having a full court enough, but then you would have had notice, that my lord mayor would have taken his barge inftead of his chair by eleven. It once occurred to me that, perhaps, fome judgment had befallen the elliptical arch at Blackfryars, and that you muft have had recourfe once again to the ingenious Mr. Smeaton, to refcue that noble pile, from being overthrown by the indignant river. In fuch cafe, to be fure, it would have been abfolutely neceffary to have paffed an immediate refolution, condemning at once the nature of the

building,

building, and the nation of the architect.
This idea, however, quickly gave way to
a more political turn of thought. I was
tempted to imagine, from the particular
time at which the court was called, that
there might be an intention of fetting the
city feal to fome inftructions for Lord
Clive, entrufting him, perhaps, with a
cordial letter for the mayor of Maxada-
vad, if in amity, or directing him to refcue the regalia of that city from the
plunder of his fcapoys, or as a matter
more peculiarly under the jurifdiction of
the common council, forbidding his
lordfhip to receive prefents from any
of the princes of the country, and re-
ftraining thofe powers which the court
of directors had extrajudicially given to
fo dangerous an extent. I improved con-
fiderably upon this hint. Satisfied as I
was of your provident care for the whole,
I determined immediately in my own
mind,

mind, that nothing lefs than the whole was the object of your prefent concern, a recefs of parliament, memorials daily prefented, the enemy as it were at our gates, who could fo properly interfere, as the ftanding council of thefe kingdoms at Guildhall affembled? I loft no time in concluding, that at leaft a petition was to be prefented, defiring immediate orders to be given for the deftruction of the French and Spanifh navy: Burn, fink, and deftroy, was to be the word, and the treaty of Paris, in fhort, to be infringed at any rate, to give Mr. P—— an opportunity of making a better peace. Seventeen hundred and fixty-four followed a little too clofe upon feventeen hundred and fixty-one. What, however, the conceptions of a working fancy were incapable of penetrating,

Volvenda dies in attulit ultro.

Saturday's

Saturday's papers fully informed me of all the particulars of the preceding day's deliberation, but efpecially of that which has occafioned the prefent addrefs to you. I mean your Chamberlain's report of Lord Chief Juftice Pratt's anfwer to the compliment paid him at the communication of your refolution with regard to his conduct, and at the prefenting him with a copy of his freedom in a gold box. As you are thought not to diflike any allufion to the proceedings of parliament you will not probably be offended with me when I tell you, *that, to prevent miftakes, I have obtained a copy of this anfwer,* the contents of which are as follow :

" S i r,

" It is impoffible for me not to feel the moft fenfible pleafure in finding my behaviour in the adminiftration of juftice approved by the city of London, — the moft refpectable body in this kingdom

2 after

after the two houses of parliament. If they have been pleafed, from any part of my conduct, to entertain an opinion of my integrity, the beft quality of a judge, my utmoft ambition is fatisfied; and I may venture, without the reproach of vanity, to take to myfelf the character of an honeft man, which the city of London have told me I am entitled to; but they will give me leave at the fame time to afcribe it only to my own good fortune, that I happen to be diftinguifhed, upon the prefent occafion, beyond the reft of my brethren; fince I am per-fuaded, that if any had been called upon as I was, they would have acted with the like confcientious regard to their oaths and to the law of the land. Since, how-ever, the city of London has now given me a reputation, I muft take more than ordinary care to preferve their gift, by the ftricteft attention to my duty, knowing that the beft way of thanking the public

for

for honours like thefe, is by perfevering
in the fame conduct, by which their approbation was firft acquired."

I have ever admired and reverenced
lord chief juftice Pratt in his judicial capacity, and I will join iffue with any
man in the warmeft commendations, of
the patience of his temper, the cogency
and perfuafion of his eloquence, and the
affability of his behaviour on the bench.
I fhall now confider him as the author
of the letter prefented to you by your
Chamberlain, in which I determine to be
decent, and if I happen to be trifling,
you muft impute it my fubject. It happens fortunately, however, and you may,
if you will, *afcribe it to my own good
fortune*, that the object of my difcuffion is
not the *obiter dictum* of a man deciding
haftily, perhaps on the fpot, what his ma-
turer thoughts might lead him to wifh it
were poffible to retract, but the cool fober

axioms

axioms of a thinking magiftrate, committed to paper, and intended for the perufal of a numerous body. The former circumftance, muft give weight, and the latter, accuracy to the compofition. In fhort, it is a *written* paper, and you are therefore competent judges, whether the deductions are unfair, or hardly ftrained; it is *written* for public perufal, drawn up, we may well fuppofe, with the utmoft temper and caution; but however drawn up, however written, it is now publici juris, under the cognizance and examination of every man who can either read himfelf, or hear it read to him.

The Letter fets out with a declaration. " It is impoffible (fays his lordfhip) for me not to feel the moft fenfible pleafure in finding my *behaviour* in the adminiftration of juftice approved by the city of London." As it cannot admit of the leaft doubt but that you meant to commend his lordfhip's behaviour, it would have

been

been lefs equivocal, if you had marked
out the fpecifick *kind* of behaviour you
intended to praife. I would juft obferve,
that there is oftentimes a wide difference
between the adminiftration of juftice, and
the *behaviour* of a particular perfon in the
adminiftration of that juftice. I have ever
conceived juftice to be eternally and im-
mutably the fame. The modes of admi-
niftring that juftice, have, to the difgrace
and the deftruction of many countries,
been fluctuating and variable. Some behaviours have been time-ferving and ob-
fequious to the will of an arbitrary mo-
narch, others corruptly influenced by the
feducing offers of lucrative advantage, others
again warped from their true bias by the
infatuating adulation of a clamorous mul-
titude; all of thefe equally wanting the
folid and permanent foundations of rec-
titude, true and impartial decifion; and
yet all of them may be called behaviours
in the adminiftration of juftice. If therefore

fore any wifh might be formed on this fubject, it fhould be, that you had been more particular in your diftinguifhing the quality of that behaviour, which you have have been fo zealous to approve: it muft be (and no one will venture to difpute it) fuch a behaviour as it becomes your dignity to commend; and yet it is hardly worth while to put your credit to the ftake, merely for the want of the addition of an epithet. But pray, how came you to be the City of London? What a bewitching thing commendation is! You are, indeed, the Common Council of the City London; but I fuppofe his lordfhip was metaphorical, and put the whole for a part.—It puts one fo in mind of Buckingham's account in the play; when he had done, fome followers of my own at the lower end of the hall hurl'd up their caps, and fome ten voices cry'd, God fave king Richard; *and thus I took the vantage of thofe few.* Thanks, gentle citizens and friends,

C 2

quoth

quoth I, this general applaufe and chearful fhout argues your wifdom and your love. Perhaps, indeed, it might be thought more creditable to be commended by the city, efpecially if we add to it the encomium which follows; " the moft refpectable body in this kingdom, *after the two houfes of parliament.*" I beg leave, gentlemen, to offer you my fincereft and moft cordial congratulations upon the diftinct allotment of your precedence, in the great fcale of the feveral bodies in Great Britain: I hope the heralds will take care to inrol it in their office books, that when you march in proceflion to St. Pauls, on the thankfgiving day for the next peace, (tho' you would neither thank God nor the king for the laft) it may regularly appear that you are to take place, next and immediately after the two houfes of parliament. No one, I think, will be hardy enough to difpute this point of chivalry with you, after it has been fettled

by

by fo folemn and legal a decifion : hither-
to, though your own rank was univerfally
conceived to be fuch as to give you the
lead of the reft of the corporations, yet
this at beft was mere matter of opinion ;
the title liable to be impugned, and no
deeds or writings authenticating this precedency ready to be produced : hencefor-
ward doubt muft give way to certainty.
Your title is good ; you have a writing to
fhew for it ; a chief juftice has given it you
under his hand, that you are the moft refpectable after the two houfes of parliament.
If this had not been the cafe (I fpeak with
the utmoft deference to his lordfhip's better judgment) there are fome bodies in
this kingdom, which I fhould have been
inclined to think had fome fort of claim
to take place of you. So ignorant am I
in every matter relating to precedency,
that I fhould have much doubted with
myfelf, whether to have allowed priority
of rank to the two houfes of convocation,

4   the

the king's moſt honourable privy council, the two famous univerſities of this
land, the great body of the law, and the
merchants a part of the city of London, who, I underſtand, are yet behind
hand in this important act of their duty,
the publick expreſſion of their approbation of his lordſhip's conduct. It might
not have been inconſiſtent, perhaps, with
the principles of ſound equity, if his lordſhip had condeſcended to have heard what
each of theſe reſpective bodies could have
urged in its behalf, in arreſt of judgment,
before he had ſo roundly diſpoſed of their
places and dignity : the convocation would
probably have pleaded the ſtation and character of their ſeveral members ; one part
of whom are by the conſtituion allowed
a ſeat in the higheſt court of judicature in
theſe kingdoms, whilſt the other is choſen
from all the eccleſiaſtical bodies of Eng-
land, repreſentatives in ſome ſort of all
the inferior clergy : they need not have
had recourſe to uſage of ancient times, by
which

which they laid taxes and impositions on their own particular body; the very writ of summons now sent out, would have been sufficient to ascertain the degree of estimation in which they have a right to be considered. The cause of their meeting is declared confessedly to be, the deliberating on the state of religion, the censuring heresies, and promoting whatever they think may tend to the honour and advancement of religion. As many therefore of you as shall think it of more importance, that a stout and well-weaponed watch be provided, than that care be taken that no new-fangled doctrines creep into the church; that globular lamps be fixed up at convenient distances, and the streets properly raked and cleansed, than that shops and houses be freed from atheistical and immoral books; so many fines paid into the chamber of London, and so many sealed proposals for buying the ofces of common hunt and water bailiff, audibly read, than that the setters forth of

ftrange

ftrange tenets be openly cenfured and re-
proved: all of you who think thus, on
the comparative ftate of the queftion, cannot hefitate a moment at afferting your
own right of precedency, before fo trifling
and infignificant a body as that of the two
houfes of convocation. Had it not been
otherwife determined, I fhould have been
tempted to imagine, that the *privy* council would have been deemed a more refpectable body than the common council
of London. And as a kind of argumen-
tum ad hominem, I could never have conceived, that his lordfhip would have fet
his hand to any affertion, which might infinuate in the leaft, that that council which
comprehends the duke of Newcaftle and
Mr. *Pitt*, could in its own nature have
the leaft grain of inferiority in its compofition. I am well aware that it may be
obferved, Mr. Pitt does not now guide the
privy council; and that whatever might
be the original inftitution of the common
council, they treat now indifcriminately of
the

the weightieft affairs of the kingdom. To which I can only anfwer, that on the 9th of November 1761, you fet a precedent exprefly againft yourfelves, by giving Mr. Pitt the lead, not only of every member of your body corporate, but even of ma- jefty itfelf; and yet he had abdicated, I will not call it the government, for that generally implies a regular, well ordered eftablifhment; but the guidance and do- minions of our affairs civil and military. The univerfities might have produced, had they been admitted to have pleaded their own caufe, fome plaufible reafons in fupport of their fuperiority, to what, if you will be called a parliament, will I fear have the epithet tacked to it, and be ftiled Parliamentum Indoctorum. But this de- cifion of his lordfhip's goes ftill farther, fo bent was he on an equitable regulation of this claim, that he nobly difdains any pre- judice in favour of a profeffion, to which he might naturally be fuppofed to lean : it is now upon record, and therefore, be it re-

D   membered,

membered, that you are more refpectable
than the great body of the law. Courts
of juftice, even the court of Common
Pleas, is allowed to be fecond to you.
No man has a fincerer veneration than
myfelf for thofe courts ; and yet, fincere
as it is, I am now taught, and a new
leffon it is that I have learnt, that the
Common Council of the city of London
has a prior claim to my regard. It is impoffible for me, indeed, as yet, to determine what operation this axiom will have
upon my mind : I have feen king, lords
and commons abufed with impunity, every
charge that malice could invent, fhot
forth againft them, without bringing the
fcandalous author of them into danger;
whilft the Moderator is a recent inftance
how very tenderly the proceedings of every
court of juftice are to be handled in public difcuffions. Who would not at the
firft blufh conclude, that our judicial powers were far fuperior, either to the legi-
flative or executive parts of our government ?

ment? And yet we are here told there is ftill a greater behind, a power ftill more refpectable than even the courts of law. Who can fee the end of this ladder of Jacob? the bottom of which indeed refts upon the ground, but the higheft part is in the clouds: and there are beings continually afcending and defcending. If the merchants had been fo ill advifed, as to put themfelves in competition on this occafion, they muft have been immediately nonfuited. That audacious act of theirs, the addreffing on the late peace, can never be forgiven them, when above twelve hundred of the moft confiderable negociants in the city, in defiance of the common council, were bold enough to thank their fovereign for having given peace to his kingdoms ; and, which was a high aggravation of the offence, to declare it to be fuch a peace, as afforded the moft reafonable grounds to believe, that the public tranquillity would be lafting. My ignorance and inexperience would have

fug-

fuggefted to me, that the feveral bodies I have mentioned might, one and all
or them, have made out very creditable
pretenfions to have taken the lead of you;
but I fubmit to his lordfhip's decifion, and
that not implicitly, my judgment is con-
vinced; I never was clearer in any pro-
pofition in my life; nay, I will go farther,
You are the moft refpectable body in this
kingdom.

Haud timeam magni dixiffe palatia cœli.

You are more refpectable than the two
houfes of parliament: and this is not a
mere gratis dictum, it can be proved from
your own authentic records; witnefs the
cyder bufinefs. Did not you (as a body
much fuperior to the legiflature) when
the two houfes of parliament concurred
in advifing the king to pafs the act for
laying a duty on cyder, think it incum-
bent on you to interpofe your conftituti-
onal authority; and as a more refpectable
                                        body

body than either lords or commons, pray the king to diffent from the advice of both houfes, to liften to the voice of his faithful commons, in common council affembled, and to refufe paffing *fo much* of the bill as related to the laying a duty upon cyder. You are more refpectable than the Commons, becaufe when they had determined that a refolution relating to the warrants was not neceffary, you, in your fuperior wifdom, thank your reprefentatives for endeavouring to obtain what you call a feafonable and parliamentary declaration. You are more refpectable than both Lords and Commons, becaufe you *affirm* what they have *difclaimed* as the privilege of parliament. You approved the motive of Mr. Wilkes's releafe from his confinement at the Tower, which the Chief Juftice of the Common Pleas directed, becaufe he was a member of the Houfe of Commons; and yet the houfe of which he was a member have folemnly declared, that privilege did not
extend

extend to the cafe ; by confequence alfo declaring, that Mr. Wilkes ought not to have been releafed. For thefe and many other reafons, which it were wafte of time to mention, it cannot furely be contefted, that feeing your jurifdiction has been fuch, as to deny, to controll, to act counter to the proceeding of the two Houfes, your confideration muft be the greater. In the next edition, therefore, of this letter, which, I fuppofe, will be at the bottom of the Chief Juftice's effigies, drawn as he is in his robes, and to be hung up in Guildhall, I would humbly fuggeft that the words, *after the two houfes of parliament,* fhould be left out, and then the city of London will confeffedly ftand, *the moft refpectable body in the kingdom.*

But to proceed : *If they have been pleafed from any part of my conduct to entertain an opinion of my integrity. If,* fays our cautious magiftrate ; and obferve, pray, how much depends upon this hypothefis ;

no lefs than the fatisfying the utmoft of his ambition. Why, Gentlemen, can it be a matter of doubt, whether you have entertained an opinion of his integrity or not? What have you been holding fo many courts and councils, paffed fo many re-folutions relative to his lordfhip's conduct, ordered the freedom of the city to be given him, defired him to fit for his picture, and after all, fhall it be liable to conteft and difpute whether you have had any opi-nion or no? Shall the Chief Juftice have actually received a copy of his freedom in a gold box, heard the Chamberlain's compliment upon it, returned him the elegant anfwer now under confideration, have fat more than once for his picture, and fhall he be the perfon to put an *if* in the fentence, and to infinuate a doubt of the reality of thefe proceedings? Talkeft thou to me of *ifs?* In any one elfe this would be rank pyrrhonifm, and the next difcuffion I fhould expect would be concerning the reality and exiftence of
the

the common council itfelf. It docs not
appear, indeed, from his lordfhip's letter,
what opinion they have entertained of his
integrity, any otherwife than may be col-
lected from the very falutary effect with
which it has been attended, I mean the
fatisfying his lordfhip's *utmoft ambition.*
If, in this free country, I might venture to
put any queftion on a man's paffions, I
fhould hefitate a little whether in ftrict
propriety the opinion of the common
council were commenfurate to fo noble an
emotion of the foul as ambition in general, doubting ftill more whether it
were capable of comprehending the full-
eft extent of that affection, whether it
could fatisfy the *utmoft* ambition, and remaining in the greateft uncertainty, whether the utmoft ambition of a chief juf-
·tice is to be fatisfied by means fo vifibly
inadequate. So totally unfkilful am I in
thefe matters, that had I been afked,
What is a judge's utmoft ambition ? I

2   fhould

should have been inconfiderate enough to have replied, in the words of the oath of office, *Juflitiam nulli vendere, nulli ne-gere, nulli differre.* In thefe turbulent days, where men are fo hurried on by the intemperance of their paffions, in fuch a manner too as to difquiet themfelves and annoy thofe about them, it is fome comfort to behold the moderation here held out to us : What muft his lordfhip's ufual tenor of defire be, when even his utmoft ambition extends no farther than to the approbation of the Common Coun-cil ? and furely no action of fo refpect-able a body can be indifferent. Every motion of theirs muft be attended with its correfpondent effect. If their opinion (whatever it be) of his integrity, apply-ing itfelf to his ambition, has given it the utmoft fatisfaction, what emotion has the giving him his *freedom* ftirred ? what paffion has the defiring him to fit for his picture fatisfied ? But I would fain know why *integrity* has fo particular an enco-

mium

mium added to it, as to be ſtyled *the beſt quality of a judge.* It cannot ſure be meant in oppoſition, much leſs in envy, of talents and ability. His lordſhip did indeed tell the city of Exeter, that he left the praiſe of capacity to others, but he never could ſurely mean to exclude himſelf from that commendation. He can never have been ſo hurt by the ſplendor of ſhining abilities as to have reſigned his pretenſions to capacity; nor much leſs would he inſinuate, that any of his brethren wanted what he calls the beſt quality of a judge. The more accurately we examine the compoſition now before us, the greater reaſon ſhall we have to admire the ſingular temper and moderation of its author. " And I may venture," ſays his lordſhip, " without the reproach of vanity, to take to myſelf the character of an honeſt man, which the city of London have told me I am entitled *to.*" For my own part, I am not much given to vanity, but, I confeſs freely, I would venture to take

to

to myfelf the character of an honeft man, whether the city of London told me fo or no. The definitions of parts, and underftanding, and judgment, are fo various and uncertain, that I might perhaps leave it to others, to decide on my pretenfions to ability, but as to integrity no one can know it fo well as myfelf; and I will venture to refer his lordfhip to a more faithful and impartial judge in this matter, than even the Common Council of London, I mean his confcience; that true, though filent monitor, will beft inform him whether he can take the character of an honeft man or no; when, therefore, he has fo good a reafon, I would not furely urge a much weaker one, the information of the city of London; or, to ufe fomewhat of a legal dialect, when I have two titles to honefty, I would reft my caufe on the ftrongeft. I would obferve juft by the way, that it is not till after his utmoft ambition has been fatisfied, that we read, his lordfhip ventures

to

to take to himfelf the chara&er of an honeft man : This would carry an infinua-
tion to thofe who are unacquainted with
his chara&er, that fo impetuous are his
paffions, fo ardent for gratification, that
they muft be fatisfied at all events, and
that when they have received that fatis-
fa&ion, then, and not till then, he ventures to call himfelf an honeft man.
However the whole of this fuppofition
immediately vanifhes, upon being ac-
quainted with the ultimatum of his de-
fires, The approbation of the city of
London, an obje& confeffedly too fmall
to hinder his purfuit after the beft quality of a judge. But why, may it be afked, does his lordfhip *now* venture to take
to himfelf the attribute of honefty. This
has, fomehow, the air of adding a no-
velty to the proceeding. Did he never
venture fo far as to call himfelf an honeft
man, even before the city of London had
told him that he was one ? or is it fo great
a piece of vanity in any one to affume that

title

title to himſelf, that it requires the authority of the Common Council to take off
the idea of oſtentation? But though his
lordſhip has been made ſo vain by the
city, in this particular, or more properly
ſpeaking, been enabled to ſupport his pretenſions to honeſty, without the reproach
of vanity; the next paragraph will make
us aſtoniſhed at his modeſty and humili-
ty. "They will give him leave to aſcribe
it only to his own good fortune, that he
happens to be diſtinguiſhed upon the preſent occaſion." Diſtinguiſhed! my good
lord. Ay, Sir, diſtinguiſhed! Evidently
referring to the preceding paragraph, the
telling his lordſhip he was an honeſt man.
Well, but how does this diſtinguiſh him?
The city does not mean to ſay, that the
chief juſtice is a *more* honeſt man than
the reſt of his brethren.

So are they all, all honourable men.

And yet I find the words, *beyond the reſt of
my brethren.* No, no; that can never be the
meaning.

meaning. Perhaps, it might be intended to fay, that it was owing to his good fortune, that his utmoft ambition had been fatisfied, and that he could take to himfelf a character, now the city of London had given it him. It is not, indeed, every man's good fortune to fee his ambition fatisfied to the utmoft extent; but when once a thing is actually given me, even were it a lefs folid body than praife and commendation, my acceptance and taking of it, I conceive, becomes the object of my choice and volition, not of chance or good fortune. Be it as it will, I am fure his lordfhip intended no reflection on his colleagues, as he declares himfelf perfuaded, that if they had been called upon as he was, they would have acted with the like confcientious regard to their oaths and to the law of the land. I moft heartily and fincerely fubfcribe to this opinion of his lordfhip's; I have not the leaft doubt, that if they had been called upon, as he fays he was, (and I am fure I am

very

very ignorant of the nature of that call) they would have conducted themfelves moft confcientioufly and faithfully. They would have been like his lordfhip in the regard to their oaths and to the laws, but I am far from being clear whether there would have been the leaft refemblance in the quality of their opinions, as I think it barely poffible they might have concurred in their fentiments as to the extent of privilege, for inftance, with the two houfes of parliament, rather than have taken up a different opinion, though fupported by the Common Council, an *obiter dictum* of Lord Holt's, and a book entitled *Twelfth Modern*, whofe authority was fully fet forth, when it was declared to be the compilation of an ignorant book-binder.

" Since, however," (as the letter goes on) " the city of London has given me a reputation, I muft take more than ordi-
                                                            nary

nary care to preferve their gift." In thefe diffolute times his lordfhip is well aware, that every motive for ftrict attention to his duty cannot be fuperfluous: all, alas, is but too little to enable the human heart to withftand the powerful temptations which affault it. If my lord's ambition, therefore, had not been already com-pleated, it muft undoubtedly have en-creafed his fatisfaction to receive fo power-ful a fpur to the performance of his obli-gations. The quality of the giver, the nature of the gift, and the manner of giving it, all confpire to awaken the at-tention and excite the induftry of the perfon who has received fo invaluable a blefling. I do not mean to depreciate either the dignity of the donors, or the worth of what has been given, I would fubmit only to you, gentlemen, fome few queries which have arifen upon this extra-ordinary Prefent.

Upon

Upon what foundation is it, by what charter are the city of London empowered to give reputations, and are they put in the fame gold boxes together with the copies of the freedom? As the city are a very polite as well as refpeƈtable body, they would never have thought of giving his lordſhip what, it may be preſumed, he was already fufficiently ſtocked with; might not, therefore, their giving him reputation, in ſome ill-difpoſed minds, raiſe a fufpicion, that before this gift, there was a deficiency, or at leaſt a diminution, which this preſent was intended to remedy? But may there not be ſome danger in thus allowing the city of London to give reputations? may they not take upon them to exercife, what would not be quite ſo amiable a part of their jurifdiƈtion; I mean the taking away again what they have thus given? And as they are a body continually fluƈtuating, what fecurity is there of their remaining in the ſentiments adopted by their

F   pre-

predeceſſors ? I would only ſubmit to
his lordſhip, whether, before he acknow-
ledged that they had given him a reputation, it would not have been adviſeable
to have aſcertained the validity of their
title to the preſentation, to have ſecured
the Preſent from all appearance of an
invidious inſinuation, and to have delibe-
rated, whether good fame, held by ſo
precarious and mutable a tenure, ſhould
be aſcribed to the diſpoſition of the Common Council? Beſides, ſurely the guilds of
Exeter and Dublin may plead ſome kind of
claim to their ſhare upon this occaſion.
The freedom and thanks they have ſo unanimouſly voted to his lordſhip cannot
but be conſidered as a ſort of underwood
rearing up and ſupporting that great pile
of reputation which, inflamed by the
breath of the city of London, has blazed
forth into all the ſeveral parts of this
kingdom. *A propos de Dublin*, I am re-
minded of a circumſtance which may,
perhaps, without the odium of a compa-
riſon,

parifon, remind you of your own proceedings. I find by Faulkner's Journal,
that the worſhipful company of Butchers
at Dublin, in common hall aſſembled,
have unanimouſly voted the freedom of
their company to Luke Lemarſh Eſq;
intendant to his Excellency the Lord
Lieutenant, for his *behaviour* in his office
during his Lordſhip's reſidence in Ire-
land. I cannot ſay, indeed, that I have
ſeen any copy of Mr. Lemarſh's anſwer
to ſo *diſtinguiſhed* a compliment; but I
cannot doubt in the leaſt, that his utmoſt ambition has been ſatisfied, and
that he will take more than ordinary
care to preſerve that reputation which
the company of butchers have given
him. I am very far, however, from being
perſuaded, that Lord Northumberland,
when he comes to audit his accounts,
or Sir M—— L—— to look them over
for him, will concur with the worſhipful butchers on this occaſion. His Excellency may be inclined to add ſtill one

freedom

freedom more to that which has already been given him, I mean perpetual freedom from his service. I proteſt ſolemnly, I do not intend the leaſt diſcourteſy to Mr. Lemaiſh, who, I dare ſay, is an honeſt worthy man (and after what the butchers have told him, will, no doubt, venture to call himſelf ſo) I would only mention, in the way of analogy, that that behaviour which recommended him ſo cordially to the butchers, might poſſibly have been ſuch as to incur the diſpleaſure of his maſter, and the contempt and diſregard of every impartial byſtander.

But to return to his lordſhip's letter, " Knowing that the beſt way of thanking the public for honours like theſe, is by perſevering in the ſame conduct by which their approbation was firſt acquired." Here, Gentlemen, is another metamorphoſis for you.——You ſat out with being the Common Council, your

next

next ſtep is a transformation into the city
of London, and now, all of a ſudden,
you are become the *Public*. The axiom
is undoubtedly a true one in this inſtance,
the ſame means which have acquired,
will preſerve ; but what are theſe means ?
are they ſuch as are fit to be openly expoſed
and avowed ? *Are they ſuch as a judge
ſhould uſe ?* What ought to be the ambition of a judge ? Ought it to be to pleaſe
any man, or any body of men, how great
or how reſpectable ſoever ? To do juſtice,
his lordſhip well knows, is a judge's
utmoſt ambition.   Warped, he ſhould
be, by no affection, no prejudice, no par-
tiality, no affectation of leaning to the
popular ſide : Such a magiſtrate will be
conſtant and inflexible in the performance
of his duty, let who will be pleaſed or
diſpleaſed. *Nec ſumit aut ponit ſecures
arbitrio popularis auræ.* And I have ſaid
this the rather, becauſe the human mind,
guarded as it is naturally againſt the
groſſer acts of corruption, by the delicacy
of

of its feelings, and by the apprehenfion
of detection, is fometimes lefs aware of
the fecret and poifonous influence of a
thirft after popular credit and eftimation:
both are equally diftant from the true and
found principles of juftice and equity,
though the latter defire is by far the moft
baneful to fociety, becaufe extending itfelf
to a greater variety of objects, and fe-
curer in its very nature from the fear of
a difcovery. You, Gentlemen, may at
your leifure, pafs fuch refolutions, with
regard to the conduct of your fuperiors,
as may feem good to you; but will the
generality of the world take their opinions
from fuch refolutions, even though fanc-
tified by the names of Bridgen at the
top, and Hodges at the bottom? If a
plain man might give you his fentiments,
you would be ferving the public much
more effentially in your fhops than in
the council. The interefts of your re-
fpective families have a ftronger tie upon
you than thofe of Great Britain. Peace and

war

war are arts and myfteries to which *you* never were apprenticed. You are not indentured to decide upon the propriety of particular taxes, nor were you ever fo much as journeymen in the great work of legiflation. Leave, therefore, with lord chief juftice Pratt, to others the praife of fhining parts and abilities; and be content yourfelves, like lord chief juftice Pratt, with the approbation of the Common Council, as the fatisfaction of your utmoft ambition.

POSTSCRIPT.

MUCH more might have been said, and in a manner somewhat more spirited and sharper. The reader will make the author's apology to himself for the omission : he will recollect, that though, by the usage of this country, any one, it should seem, may abuse the C——n, and the C——n C——l in particular, may say what they please against the proceedings of both houses of ———— with impunity, yet it is against the liberty of the subject to glance in the least at the C—— j——, I mean of the C—— P——. From usage it appears, that

the

the law is different with refpect to the
C—— J—— of the K—— B——,
and that it is even commendable and
patriotic to vent whatever paffion or
malice may fuggeft againft him.

F I N I S.

www.ingramcontent.com/pod-product-compliance
Lightning Source LLC
Chambersburg PA
CBHW021441090426
42739CB00009B/1582